Vegan Cookbook for Moms

Quick, Delicious & Clean Meals on a Budget

By Tammy Thun

Sommario

Introduction

Vegetarianism refers to a lifestyle that excludes the consumption of all forms of meat, including pork, chicken, beef, lamb, venison, fish and shells.

According to the preference and belief of different people different degrees of vegetarianism were born, in fact there are some people who like to use at least animal derivatives and others who instead take their beliefs to the extreme by eliminating even the derivatives and are called vegans.

Vegetarianism as well as being a beautiful mission of life and demonstration of respect for nature is also good for the respect of our bodies by reducing the risk of chronic diseases.

Have fun with our fantastic recipes

Main course

Spaghetti with Butterbeans and Ricotta

Ingredients

1 yellow onion, medium chopped 1 red bell pepper, chopped

15 ounce can butterbeans, rinsed and drained 15 ounce can black beans , rinsed and drained 28 ounce crushed tomatoes

4 tbsp. vegan cream cheese 1 tsp. herbs de Provence

½ teaspoon salt

1/8 teaspoon black pepper 2 cups vegetable stock

8 ounces spaghetti uncooked 1 ½ cups Ricotta Cheese Garnishing ingredients:

chopped green onions for serving

Put all of the ingredients except for pasta, vegan cheese, and garnishing ingredients in your slow cooker.

Combine and cover.

Cook on high heat for 4 hours or low heat for 7 hours.

Add the pasta and cooking on high heat for 18 minutes, or until pasta becomes al dente

Add 1 cup of cheese and stir.

Sprinkle with the remaining ricotta cheese and garnishing ingredients

Spaghetti with Chorizo and Mozarella

Ingredients

1 red onion, medium chopped 1 green bell pepper chopped 15 ounce can kidney beans

15 ounce can great northern beans28 ounce crushed tomatoes

1/4 cup vegan chorizos, coarsely chopped1 tsp. dried thyme

½ teaspoon salt

1/8 teaspoon black pepper2 cups vegetable stock

8 ounces spaghetti noodles uncooked 1 ½ cups Mozarella Cheese Garnishing ingredients:

chopped green onions for serving

Put all of the ingredients except for pasta, mozarella cheese, andgarnishing ingredients in your slow cooker.

Combine and cover.

Cook on high heat for 4 hours or low heat for 7 hours.

Add the pasta and cooking on high heat for 18 minutes, or until pastabecomes al dente

Add 1 cup of cheese and stir.

Sprinkle with the remaining mozarella cheese and garnishingingredients

Pappardelle Pasta with Tomatoes and Garbanzo Beans

Ingredients

1 red onion, medium chopped1 green bell pepper chopped

15 ounce can butterbeans, rinsed and drained

15 ounce can garbanzo beans , rinsed and drained28 ounce crushed tomatoes

2 tbsp. tomato paste1 tsp. basil

1 tsp. Italian seasoning

½ teaspoon salt

1/8 teaspoon black pepper2 cups vegetable stock

8 ounces pappardelle pasta uncooked 1 ½ cups Vegan Cheese

(Tofu   Based)   Garnishing
ingredients:

chopped green onions for serving

Put all of the ingredients except for pasta, vegan cheese, andgarnishing ingredients in your slow cooker.

Combine and cover.

Cook on high heat for 4 hours or low heat for 7 hours.

Add the pasta and cooking on high heat for 18 minutes, or until pastabecomes al dente

Add 1 cup of cheese and stir.

Sprinkle with the remaining vegan cheese and garnishing ingredients

Macaroni and Pepper Jack Cheese

Ingredients

15 ounce can lima beans rinsed and drained

15 ounce can garbanzo beans rinsed and drained 28 ounce crushed tomatoes

4 tbsp. pesto

1 tsp. Italian seasoning

½ teaspoon salt

1/8 teaspoon black pepper 2 cups vegetable stock

8 ounces whole wheat elbow macaroni pasta uncooked 1 ½ cups Pepper Jack Cheese

Garnishing ingredients:

chopped green onions for serving

Put all of the ingredients except for pasta, cheese, and garnishing ingredients in your slow cooker.

Combine and cover.

Cook on high heat for 4 hours or low heat for 7 hours.

Add the pasta and cooking on high heat for 18 minutes, or until pasta becomes al dente

Add 1 cup of cheese and stir.

Sprinkle with the remaining cheese and garnishing ingredients

Farfalle Pasta in Spicy Chimichurri Sauce with Ricotta

Ingredients

5 jalapeno peppers

1 yellow onion, chopped

15 ounce can butterbeans, rinsed and drained

15 ounce can borlotti beans , rinsed and drained4 tbsp. chimichurri sauce

1/2 tsp. cayenne pepper

½ teaspoon salt

1/8 teaspoon black pepper 2 cups vegetable stock

8 ounces farfalle pasta uncooked

1 ½ cups Ricotta Cheese Garnishing ingredients:chopped green onions for serving

Put all of the ingredients except for pasta, vegan cheese, andgarnishing ingredients in your slow cooker.

Combine and cover.

Cook on high heat for 4 hours or low heat for 7 hours.

Add the pasta and cooking on high heat for 18 minutes, or until pastabecomes al dente

Add 1 cup of cheese and stir.

Sprinkle with the remaining cheese and garnishing ingredients

Elbow Macaroni with Cream Cheese and Mozarella

Ingredients

1   red   onion,   medium

chopped 1 green bell pepper chopped 15 ounce can kidney beans 15 ounce can lima beans

28 ounce crushed tomatoes 3 ounces vegan mozzarella 1 tsp. Italian seasoning

½ teaspoon salt

1/8 teaspoon black pepper 2 cups vegetable stock

8 ounces whole wheat elbow macaroni pasta uncooked 1 ½ cups Cream Cheese

Garnishing ingredients:

chopped green onions for serving

Put all of the ingredients except for pasta, vegan cheese, and garnishing ingredients in your slow cooker.

Combine and cover.

Cook on high heat for 4 hours or low heat for 7 hours.

Add the pasta and cooking on high heat for 18 minutes, or until pastabecomes al dente

Add 1 cup of cheese and stir.

Sprinkle with the remaining cheese and garnishing ingredients

Spaghetti with Green Olives and Tomatoes

Ingredients

1 red onion, medium chopped 1 green bell pepper chopped 28 ounce crushed tomatoes 1/4 cup green olives

2 tbsp. capers

½ teaspoon salt

1/8 teaspoon black pepper 2 cups vegetable stock

8 ounces spaghetti noodles uncooked 1 ½ cups Vegan Cheese (Tofu Based) Garnishing ingredients:

chopped green onions for serving

Put all of the ingredients except for pasta, vegan cheese, andgarnishing ingredients in your slow cooker.

Combine and cover.

Cook on high heat for 4 hours or low heat for 7 hours.

Add the pasta and cooking on high heat for 18 minutes, or until pastabecomes al dente

Add 1 cup of cheese and stir.

Sprinkle with the remaining vegan cheese and garnishing ingredients

Whole Wheat Macaroni With Mozzarella and Parmesan Cheese

Ingredients

1 red onion, medium chopped1 green bell pepper chopped 28 ounce crushed tomatoes

4 tbsp. vegan cream cheese 1 tsp. herbs de Provence

½ teaspoon salt

1/8 teaspoon black pepper 2 cups vegetable stock

8 ounces whole wheat elbow macaroni pasta uncooked1 cups Mozarella Cheese

½ cup parmesan cheese Garnishing ingredients:

chopped green onions for serving

Put all of the ingredients except for pasta, vegan cheese, and garnishing ingredients in your slow cooker.

Combine and cover.

Cook on high heat for 4 hours or low heat for 7 hours.

Add the pasta and cooking on high heat for 18 minutes, or until pasta becomes al dente

Add 1 cup of mozzarella cheese and stir.

Sprinkle with the remaining parmesan cheese and garnishing ingredients

Penne Pasta with Chorizo and Pecorino Romano

Ingredients

1 red onion, medium chopped 28 ounce crushed tomatoes

1/4 cup vegan chorizos, coarsely chopped 1 tsp. dried thyme

½ teaspoon salt

1/8 teaspoon black pepper 2 cups vegetable stock

8 ounces penne pasta uncooked

½ cup Pecorino Romano Cheese

½ cup Mozarella cheese

½ cup cheddar cheese Garnishing ingredients:

chopped green onions for serving

Put all of the ingredients except for pasta, vegan cheese, andgarnishing ingredients in your slow cooker.

Combine and cover.

Cook on high heat for 4 hours or low heat for 7 hours.

Add the pasta and cooking on high heat for 18 minutes, or until pastabecomes al dente

Add 1/2 cup of mozzarella cheese & ½ cup of cheddar cheese and stir.

Sprinkle with the remaining pecorino romano cheese and garnishingingredients

Papardelle Pasta with Cheddar Cheese

Ingredients

1 red onion, medium chopped 1 green bell pepper chopped

15 ounce can fava beans, rinsed and drained 15 ounce can navy beans, rinsed and drained 28 ounce crushed tomatoes

4 tbsp. pesto

1 tsp. Italian seasoning

½ teaspoon salt

1/8 teaspoon black pepper 2 cups vegetable stock

8 ounces pappardelle pasta uncooked 1 ¼ cups Mozarella Cheese

¼ cup Cheddar Cheese Garnishing ingredients:

chopped green onions for serving

Put all of the ingredients except for pasta, vegan cheese, andgarnishing ingredients in your slow cooker.

Combine and cover.

Cook on high heat for 4 hours or low heat for 7 hours.

Add the pasta and cooking on high heat for 18 minutes, or until pastabecomes al dente

Add 1 cup of mozzarella cheese and stir.

Sprinkle with the remaining cheese and garnishing ingredients

Slow Cooked Fettuccini with Mozarella

Ingredients

1 red onion, medium chopped 1 green bell pepper chopped 15 ounce sour cream

28 ounce crushed tomatoes 2 tbsp. tomato paste

1 tsp. basil

1 tsp. Italian seasoning

½ teaspoon salt

1/8 teaspoon black pepper 2 cups vegetable stock

8 ounces fettuccini uncooked

1 ½ cups Mozarella Cheese (Tofu

Based)Garnishing ingredients:

chopped green onions for serving

Put all of the ingredients except for pasta, vegan cheese, andgarnishing ingredients in your slow cooker.

Combine and cover.

Cook on high heat for 4 hours or low heat for 7 hours.

Add the pasta and cooking on high heat for 18 minutes, or until pastabecomes al dente

Add 1 cup of mozzarella cheese and stir.

Sprinkle with the remaining cheese and garnishing ingredients

Pasta Shells in Chimichurri Sauce with Cream Cheese

Ingredients

5 jalapeno peppers

4 tbsp. chimichurri
sauce 1/2 tsp. cayenne

pepper

½ teaspoon salt

1/8 teaspoon black pepper 2 cups vegetable stock

8 ounces pasta shells uncooked 1 ½ cups Cream Cheese Garnishing ingredients:

chopped green onions for serving

Put all of the ingredients except for pasta, vegan cheese, andgarnishing ingredients in your slow cooker.

Combine and cover.

Cook on high heat for 4 hours or low heat for 7 hours.

Add the pasta and cooking on high heat for 18 minutes, or until pastabecomes al dente

Add 1 cup of cheese and stir.

Sprinkle with the remaining cheese and garnishing ingredients

Farfalle Pasta with Ricotta Cheese

Ingredients

1 yellow onion, medium chopped 1 red bell pepper, chopped

28 ounce canned green tomatoes 1/4 cup green olives

2 tbsp. capers

½ teaspoon salt

1/8 teaspoon black pepper 2 cups vegetable stock

8 ounces farfalle pasta uncooked 1 ½ cups Ricotta Cheese Garnishing ingredients:

chopped green onions for serving

Put all of the ingredients except for pasta, vegan cheese, andgarnishing ingredients in your slow cooker.

Combine and cover.

Cook on high heat for 4 hours or low heat for 7 hours.

Add the pasta and cooking on high heat for 18 minutes, or until pastabecomes al dente

Add 1 cup of cheese and stir.

Sprinkle with the remaining ricotta cheese and garnishing ingredients

Spaghetti with Pepper Jack Cheese and Mozarella

Ingredients

1 red onion, medium chopped 1 green bell pepper chopped

14 ounce crushed green tomatoes 14 ounce crushed tomatoes

3 ounces vegan mozzarella 1 tsp. Italian seasoning

½ teaspoon salt

1/8 teaspoon black pepper 2 cups vegetable stock

8 ounces spaghetti noodles uncooked

1 ½ cups Pepper Jack Cheese , shredded Garnishing ingredients:

chopped green onions for serving

Put all of the ingredients except for pasta, vegan cheese, and garnishing ingredients in your slow cooker.

Combine and cover.

Cook on high heat for 4 hours or low heat for 7 hours.

Add the pasta and cooking on high heat for 18 minutes, or until pasta becomes al dente

Add 1 cup of pepper jack cheese and stir.

Sprinkle with the remaining pepper jack cheese and garnishing ingredients

Spicy Macaroni and Mozarella Cheese

Ingredients

¼ cup extra virgin olive oil i1 red onion

28 ounce crushed tomatoes

½ teaspoon salt

1/8 teaspoon black pepper 2 cups vegetable stock

8 ounces whole wheat elbow macaroni pasta uncooked 1 ¼ cups Mozarella Cheese (Tofu Based)

¼ cup Parmigiano Regiano Cheese Garnishing ingredients:

chopped green onions for serving

Put all of the ingredients except for pasta, vegan cheese, and garnishing ingredients in your slow cooker.

Combine and cover.

Cook on high heat for 4 hours or low heat for 7 hours.

Add the pasta and cooking on high heat for 18 minutes, or until pastabecomes al dente

Add 1 cup of cheese and stir.

Sprinkle with the remaining vegan cheese and garnishing ingredients

Penne Pasta with Pesto and Mozarella

Ingredients

1 red onion, medium chopped 1 green bell pepper chopped

15 ounce can lima beans, rinsed and drained 15 ounce can soy beans, rinsed and drained 28 ounce crushed tomatoes

4 tbsp. pesto

1 tsp. Italian seasoning

½ teaspoon salt

1/8 teaspoon black pepper 2 cups vegetable stock

8 ounces penne pasta uncooked 1 ½ cups Mozarella Cheese Garnishing ingredients:

chopped green onions for serving

Put all of the ingredients except for pasta, vegan cheese, and garnishing ingredients in your slow cooker.

Combine and cover.

Cook on high heat for 4 hours or low heat for 7 hours.

Add the pasta and cooking on high heat for 18 minutes, or until pasta becomes al dente

Add 1 cup of cheese and stir.

Sprinkle with the remaining cheese and garnishing ingredients

Pappardelle Pasta with Mozarella Cheese

Ingredients

1 red onion, medium chopped

15 ounce can lima beans, rinsed and drained

15 ounce can borlotti beans , rinsed and drained28 ounce crushed tomatoes

4 tbsp. cream cheese

1 tsp. herbs de Provence

½ teaspoon salt

1/8 teaspoon black pepper2 cups vegetable stock

8 ounces pappardelle pasta uncooked 1 ½ cups mozarella Cheese Garnishing ingredients:

chopped green onions for serving

Put all of the ingredients except for pasta, vegan cheese, and garnishing ingredients in your slow cooker.

Combine and cover.

Cook on high heat for 4 hours or low heat for 7 hours.

Add the pasta and cooking on high heat for 18 minutes, or until pasta becomes al dente

Add 1 cup of mozzarella cheese and stir.

Sprinkle with the remaining cream cheese, mozzarella cheese and garnishing ingredients

Macaroni and Mozarella and Monterey Jack Cheese

Ingredients

1 yellow onion, medium chopped 28 ounce crushed tomatoes

1/4 cup vegan chorizos, coarsely chopped 1 tsp. dried thyme

½ teaspoon salt

1/8 teaspoon black
pepper 2 cups vegetable
stock

8 ounces whole wheat elbow macaroni pasta
uncooked 1 ½ cups Mozarella Cheese

½ cup Monterey Jack
Cheese Garnishing
ingredients:

chopped green onions for serving

Put all of the ingredients except for pasta, vegan cheese,
and garnishing ingredients in your slow cooker.

Combine and cover.

Cook on high heat for 4 hours or low heat for 7 hours.

Add the pasta and cooking on high heat for 18 minutes, or until
pasta becomes al dente

Add 1 cup of cheese and stir.

Sprinkle with the remaining vegan cheese and garnishing ingredients

Pasta Shells with Chimichurri Sauce and Gouda Cheese

Ingredients

1 red onion, medium chopped 5 jalapeno peppers

1 red onion

4 tbsp. chimichurri sauce 1/2 tsp. cayenne pepper

½ teaspoon salt

1/8 teaspoon black pepper 2 cups vegetable stock

8 ounces pasta shells uncooked

1 ½ cups gouda cheese (Tofu Based) Garnishing ingredients:

chopped green onions for serving

Put all of the ingredients except for pasta, vegan cheese, andgarnishing ingredients in your slow cooker.

Combine and cover.

Cook on high heat for 4 hours or low heat for 7 hours.

Add the pasta and cooking on high heat for 18 minutes, or until pastabecomes al dente

Add 1 cup of cheese and stir.

Sprinkle with the remaining cheese and garnishing ingredients

Farfalle with Capers

Ingredients

1 red onion, medium chopped 1 green bell pepper chopped

15 ounce can lima beans, rinsed and drained 15 ounce can red beans, rinsed and drained 28 ounce crushed tomatoes

1/4 cup green olives 2 tbsp. capers

½ teaspoon salt

1/8 teaspoon black pepper 2 cups vegetable stock

8 ounces farfalle pasta uncooked

1 ½ cups Vegan Cheese (Tofu Based)

Garnishing ingredients:

chopped green onions for serving

Put all of the ingredients except for pasta, vegan cheese, andgarnishing ingredients in your slow cooker.

Combine and cover.

Cook on high heat for 4 hours or low heat for 7 hours.

Add the pasta and cooking on high heat for 18 minutes, or until pastabecomes al dente

Add 1 cup of cheese and stir.

Sprinkle with the remaining vegan cheese and garnishing ingredients

Penne Pasta with Mozarella and Gorgonzola Cheese

Ingredients

1 red onion, medium chopped 28 ounce crushed tomatoes

3 ounces vegan mozzarella 1 tsp. Italian seasoning

½ teaspoon salt

1/8 teaspoon black pepper 2 cups vegetable stock

8 ounces penne pasta uncooked 1 ½ cups mozzarella Cheese

¼ cup Gorgonzola cheese Garnishing ingredients:

chopped green onions for serving

Put all of the ingredients except for pasta, vegan cheese, andgarnishing ingredients in your slow cooker.

Combine and cover.

Cook on high heat for 4 hours or low heat for 7 hours.

Add the pasta and cooking on high heat for 18 minutes, or until pastabecomes al dente

Add 1 cup of cheese and stir.

Sprinkle with the remaining vegan cheese and garnishing ingredients

Fettuccini with Pinto Beans and Cheddar Cheese

Ingredients

1 red onion, medium chopped 1 green bell pepper chopped 8 cloves garlic, minced

28 ounce crushed tomatoes 4 tbsp. vegan cream cheese 1 tsp. herbs de Provence

½ teaspoon salt

1/8 teaspoon black pepper 2 cups vegetable stock

8 ounces fettuccini uncooked 1 ½ cups Cheddar Cheese Garnishing ingredients:

chopped green onions for serving

Put all of the ingredients except for pasta, vegan cheese, andgarnishing ingredients in your slow cooker.

Combine and cover.

Cook on high heat for 4 hours or low heat for 7 hours.

Add the pasta and cooking on high heat for 18 minutes, or until pastabecomes al dente

Add 1 cup of cheese and stir.

Sprinkle with the remaining cheese and garnishing ingredients

Spaghetti with Kalamata Olives

Ingredients

1 red onion, medium chopped

¼ cup kalamata olives

28 ounce crushed tomatoes4 tbsp. pesto

1 tsp. Italian seasoning

½ teaspoon salt

1/8 teaspoon black pepper 2 cups vegetable stock

8 ounces spaghetti noodles uncooked 1 ½ cups Vegan Cheese (Tofu Based) Garnishing ingredients:

chopped green onions for serving

Put all of the ingredients except for pasta, vegan cheese, andgarnishing ingredients in your slow cooker.

Combine and cover.

Cook on high heat for 4 hours or low heat for 7 hours.

Add the pasta and cooking on high heat for 18 minutes, or until pasta becomes al dente

Add 1 cup of cheese and stir.

Sprinkle with the remaining cheese and garnishing ingredients

Papardelle Pasta and Gouda Cheese

Ingredients

1 yellow onion, medium chopped 1 red bell pepper, chopped

28 ounce crushed green tomatoes 2 tbsp. tomato paste

1 tsp. basil

1 tsp. Italian seasoning

½ teaspoon salt

1/8 teaspoon black pepper 2 cups vegetable stock

8 ounces pappardelle pasta uncooked 1 ½ cups gouda cheese

Garnishing ingredients:

chopped green onions for serving

Put all of the ingredients except for pasta, vegan cheese, andgarnishing ingredients in your slow cooker.

Combine and cover.

Cook on high heat for 4 hours or low heat for 7 hours.

Add the pasta and cooking on high heat for 18 minutes, or until pastabecomes al dente

Add 1 cup of cheese and stir.

Sprinkle with the remaining gouda cheese and garnishingingredients

Elbow Macaroni with Vegan Chorizo and Green Olives

Ingredients

1 red onion, medium chopped 1 green bell pepper chopped

½ cup green olives, drained 9 cloves garlic, minced

28 ounce crushed tomatoes

1/4 cup vegan chorizos, coarsely chopped 1 tsp. dried thyme

½ teaspoon salt

1/8 teaspoon black pepper 2 cups vegetable stock

8 ounces whole wheat elbow macaroni pasta uncooked 1 ½ cups Mozzarella Cheese

Garnishing ingredients:

chopped green onions for serving

Put all of the ingredients except for pasta, vegan cheese, andgarnishing ingredients in your slow cooker.

Combine and cover.

Cook on high heat for 4 hours or low heat for 7 hours.

Add the pasta and cooking on high heat for 18 minutes, or until pastabecomes al dente

Add 1 cup of cheese and stir.

Sprinkle with the remaining mozarella cheese and garnishingingredients

Pasta Shells with Cheddar Cheese and Capers

Ingredients

1 red onion, medium chopped 1 green bell pepper chopped

¼ cup capers, drained

4 tbsp. chimichurri sauce 1/2 tsp. cayenne pepper

½ teaspoon salt

1/8 teaspoon black pepper 2 cups vegetable stock

8 ounces pasta shells uncooked 1 ½ cups Cheddar Cheese Garnishing ingredients:

chopped green onions for serving

Put all of the ingredients except for pasta, vegan cheese, andgarnishing ingredients in your slow cooker.

Combine and cover.

Cook on high heat for 4 hours or low heat for 7 hours.

Add the pasta and cooking on high heat for 18 minutes, or until pastabecomes al dente

Add 1 cup of cheese and stir.

Sprinkle with the remaining cheese and garnishing ingredients

Penne Pasta with Olives and Cream Cheese

Ingredients

1 red onion, medium chopped 1 green bell pepper chopped

¼ cup olives, drained

¼ cup capers, drained

28 ounce crushed tomatoes 4 tbsp. cream cheese

1 tsp. herbs de Provence

½ teaspoon salt

1/8 teaspoon black pepper 2 cups vegetable stock

8 ounces penne pasta uncooked 1 ½ cups mozzarella

cheese Garnishing ingredients:

chopped green onions for serving

Put all of the ingredients except for pasta, vegan cheese, andgarnishing ingredients in your slow cooker.

Combine and cover.

Cook on high heat for 4 hours or low heat for 7 hours.

Add the pasta and cooking on high heat for 18 minutes, or until pastabecomes al dente

Add 1 cup of cheese and stir.

Sprinkle with the remaining vegan cheese and garnishing ingredients

Elbow Macaroni with Olives and Capers

Ingredients

1 red onion, medium chopped

15 ounce can button mushrooms 28 ounce crushed tomatoes

1/4 cup green olives 2 tbsp. capers

½ teaspoon salt

1/8 teaspoon black pepper 2 cups vegetable stock

8 ounces whole wheat elbow macaroni pasta uncooked 1 ½ cups Vegan Cheese (Tofu Based)

Garnishing ingredients:

chopped green onions for serving

Put all of the ingredients except for pasta, cheese, and garnishingingredients in your slow cooker.

Combine and cover.

Cook on high heat for 4 hours or low heat for 7 hours.

Add the pasta and cooking on high heat for 18 minutes, or until pastabecomes al dente

Add 1 cup of cheese and stir.

Sprinkle with the remaining vegan cheese and garnishing ingredients

Farfalle Pasta with Mozarella and Capers

Ingredients

1 yellow onion, medium chopped

¼ cup capers, drained

28 ounce crushed
tomatoes 3 ounces vegan
mozzarella 1 tsp. Italian

seasoning

½ teaspoon salt

1/8 teaspoon black pepper2 cups vegetable stock

8 ounces farfalle pasta uncooked

1 ½ cups Vegan Cheese (Tofu Based)Garnishing ingredients:

chopped green onions for serving

Put all of the ingredients except for pasta, cheese, and garnishingingredients in your slow cooker.

Combine and cover.

Cook on high heat for 4 hours or low heat for 7 hours.

Add the pasta and cooking on high heat for 18 minutes, or until pastabecomes al dente

Add 1 cup of cheese and stir.

Sprinkle with the remaining vegan cheese and garnishing ingredients

Elbow Macaroni with Crimini Mushrooms

Ingredients

1 red onion, medium chopped

¼ cup button mushrooms, drained

¼ cup cremini mushrooms
15 ounce can tomato
sauce 28 ounce crushed
tomatoes4 tbsp. pesto

1 tsp. Italian seasoning

½ teaspoon salt

1/8 teaspoon black
pepper 2 cups vegetable
stock

8 ounces whole wheat elbow macaroni pasta
uncooked1 ½ cups Mozarella Cheese

Garnishing ingredients:

chopped green onions for serving

Put all of the ingredients except for pasta, cheese, and garnishing ingredients in your slow cooker.

Combine and cover.

Cook on high heat for 4 hours or low heat for 7 hours.

Add the pasta and cooking on high heat for 18 minutes, or until pasta becomes al dente

Add 1 cup of cheese and stir.

Sprinkle with the remaining mozarella cheese and garnishing ingredients

Spaghetti with Oyster Mushrooms

Ingredients

1 red onion, medium chopped

¼ cup oyster mushrooms 15 ounce tomato sauce

28 ounce crushed tomatoes 2 tbsp. tomato paste

1 tsp. basil

1 tsp. Italian seasoning

½ teaspoon salt

1/8 teaspoon black pepper 2 cups vegetable stock

8 ounces spaghetti noodles uncooked 1 ½ cups Vegan Cheese

(Tofu Based) Garnishing ingredients:

chopped green onions for serving

Put all of the ingredients except for pasta, cheese, and garnishingingredients in your slow cooker.

Combine and cover.

Cook on high heat for 4 hours or low heat for 7 hours.

Add the pasta and cooking on high heat for 18 minutes, or until pastabecomes al dente

Add 1 cup of cheese and stir.

Sprinkle with the remaining vegan cheese and garnishing ingredients

Papardelle Pasta and Oyster Mushroom and Vegan Chorizo

Ingredients

1 red onion, medium chopped 15 ounce tomato sauce

¼ cup oyster mushrooms, drained 28 ounce crushed tomatoes

1/4 cup vegan chorizos, coarsely chopped 1 tsp. dried thyme

½ teaspoon salt

1/8 teaspoon black pepper 2 cups vegetable stock

8 ounces pappardelle pasta uncooked 1 ½ cups Vegan Cheese (Tofu Based) Garnishing ingredients:

chopped green onions for serving

Put all of the ingredients except for pasta, vegan cheese, andgarnishing ingredients in your slow cooker.

Combine and cover.

Cook on high heat for 4 hours or low heat for 7 hours.

Add the pasta and cooking on high heat for 18 minutes, or until pastabecomes al dente

Add 1 cup of cheese and stir.

Sprinkle with the remaining vegan cheese and garnishing ingredients

Penne Pasta with Green Tomatoes in Chimichurri Sauce

Ingredients

1 red onion, medium chopped

1/4 cup vegan Italian sausage, coarsely chopped 1 cup green tomatoes chopped

¼ cup capers, drained

4 tbsp. chimichurri sauce 1/2 tsp. cayenne pepper

½ teaspoon salt

1/8 teaspoon black pepper 2 cups vegetable stock

8 ounces penne pasta uncooked

1 ½ cups Vegan Cheese (Tofu Based) Garnishing ingredients:

chopped green onions for serving

Put all of the ingredients except for pasta, vegan cheese, andgarnishing ingredients in your slow cooker.

Combine and cover.

Cook on high heat for 4 hours or low heat for 7 hours.

Add the pasta and cooking on high heat for 18 minutes, or until pastabecomes al dente

Add 1 cup of cheese and stir.

Sprinkle with the remaining vegan cheese and garnishing ingredients

Creamy Elbow Mac and Vegan Italian Sausage

Ingredients

1 red onion, medium chopped

1/4 cup vegan Italian sausage, coarsely chopped 1 cup oyster mushrooms

15 ounce can tomato sauce 28 ounce crushed tomatoes 4 tbsp. vegan cream cheese 1 tsp. herbs de Provence

½ teaspoon salt

1/8 teaspoon black pepper 2 cups vegetable stock

8 ounces whole wheat elbow macaroni pasta uncooked 1 ½ cups Vegan Cheese (Tofu Based)

Garnishing ingredients:

chopped green onions for serving

Put all of the ingredients except for pasta, vegan cheese, andgarnishing ingredients in your slow cooker.

Combine and cover.

Cook on high heat for 4 hours or low heat for 7 hours.

Add the pasta and cooking on high heat for 18 minutes, or until pastabecomes al dente

Add 1 cup of cheese and stir.

Sprinkle with the remaining vegan cheese and garnishing ingredients

Farfalle Pasta with Vegan Cream Cheese Tomato Sauce

Ingredients

1 yellow onion, medium
chopped 1 green bell pepper,
chopped

8 ounces, vegan cream cheese 15 ounce tomato sauce

28 ounce crushed tomatoes 1/4 cup green olives

2 tbsp. capers

½ teaspoon salt

1/8 teaspoon black pepper 2 cups vegetable stock

8 ounces farfalle pasta uncooked

1 ½ cups Vegan Cheese (Tofu Based) Garnishing ingredients:

chopped green onions for serving

Put all of the ingredients except for pasta, vegan cheese, andgarnishing ingredients in your slow cooker.

Combine and cover.

Cook on high heat for 4 hours or low heat for 7 hours.

Add the pasta and cooking on high heat for 18 minutes, or until pastabecomes al dente

Add 1 cup of cheese and stir.

Sprinkle with the remaining vegan cheese and garnishing ingredients

Pasta Shells with Tomato Sauce and Ricotta Cheese

Ingredients

1 red onion, medium chopped 15 ounce can tomato sauce 28 ounce crushed tomatoes

3 ounces vegan mozzarella 1 tsp. Italian seasoning

½ teaspoon salt

1/8 teaspoon black pepper 2 cups vegetable stock

8 ounces pasta shells uncooked 1 ½ cups Ricotta Cheese Garnishing ingredients:

chopped green onions for serving

Put all of the ingredients except for pasta, vegan cheese, andgarnishing ingredients in your slow cooker.

Combine and cover.

Cook on high heat for 4 hours or low heat for 7 hours.

Add the pasta and cooking on high heat for 18 minutes, or until pastabecomes al dente

Add 1 cup of Ricotta cheese and stir.

Sprinkle with the remaining vegan cheese and garnishing ingredients

Elbow Macaroni with Mozarella and Gorgonzola Cheese

Ingredients

1 red onion, medium chopped

1/4 cup vegan Italian sausage, coarsely chopped

¼ cup red pesto

15 ounce can tomato sauce 28 ounce crushed tomatoes 2 tbsp. tomato paste

1 tsp. basil

1 tsp. Italian seasoning

½ teaspoon salt

1/8 teaspoon black pepper 2 cups vegetable stock

8 ounces whole wheat elbow macaroni pasta uncooked 1 ½ cups Mozarella Cheese

¼ cup gorgonzola cheese Garnishing ingredients:

chopped green onions for serving

Put all of the ingredients except for pasta, vegan cheese, and garnishing ingredients in your slow cooker.

Combine and cover.

Cook on high heat for 4 hours or low heat for 7 hours.

Add the pasta and cooking on high heat for 18 minutes, or until pasta becomes al dente

Add 1 cup of cheese and stir.

Sprinkle with the remaining vegan cheese and garnishing ingredients

Papardelle Pasta with Ricotta Cheese

Ingredients

1 red onion, medium chopped 28 ounce crushed tomatoes

4 tbsp. pesto

4 tbsp. red pesto

1 tsp. Italian seasoning

½ teaspoon salt

1/8 teaspoon black pepper 2 cups vegetable stock

8 ounces pappardelle pasta uncooked 1 ½ cups Ricotta Cheese

Garnishing ingredients:

chopped green onions for serving

Put all of the ingredients except for pasta, vegan cheese, andgarnishing ingredients in your slow cooker.

Combine and cover.

Cook on high heat for 4 hours or low heat for 7 hours.

Add the pasta and cooking on high heat for 18 minutes, or until pastabecomes al dente

Add 1 cup of cheese and stir.

Sprinkle with the remaining cheese and garnishing ingredients

Penne Pasta with Capers and Vegan Chorizo

Ingredien

ts 1 ancho chili

1 tsp. Tabasco hot sauce 1 red onion

15 ounce can tomato sauce

¼ cup capers, drained

28 ounce crushed tomatoes

1/4 cup vegan chorizos, coarsely chopped 1 tsp. dried thyme

½ teaspoon salt

1/8 teaspoon black pepper 2 cups vegetable stock

8 ounces penne pasta uncooked

1 ½ cups Mozarella Cheese (Tofu

Based)Garnishing ingredients:

chopped green onions for serving

Put all of the ingredients except for pasta, vegan cheese, andgarnishing ingredients in your slow cooker.

Combine and cover.

Cook on high heat for 4 hours or low heat for 7 hours.

Add the pasta and cooking on high heat for 18 minutes, or until pastabecomes al dente

Add 1 cup of cheese and stir.

Sprinkle with the remaining cheese and garnishing ingredients

Lima Beans with Quinoa

Ingredients

6 green bell peppers

1 cup uncooked quinoa, rinsed

1 14 ounce can garbanzo beans, rinsed and drained 1 14 ounce can lima beans

1 1/2 cups red enchilada sauce 2 tbsp. tomato paste

1 tsp. basil

1 tsp. Italian seasoning

1/2 teaspoon garlic powder

½ tsp. sea salt

1 1/2 cups shredded mozzarella cheese Toppings: cilantro, avocado.

Cut out the stems of the bell pepper. Take out the ribs and

the seeds.

Mix the quinoa, beans, enchilada sauce, spices, and 1 cup of thevegan cheese thoroughly.

Fill each pepper with the quinoa and bean mixture. Pour half a cup water to the slow cooker.

Place the peppers in the slow cooker (partially submerged in thewater).

Cover and cook on low heat for 6 hours or high heat for 3 hours. Uncover and distribute the remaining vegan cheese over the tops ofthe peppers, and cover for a 4 to 5 minutes to melt the cheese.

Top with cilantro & avocado

Vegetarian Bolognese

Ingredients

1 large sweet red onion, diced 2 carrots, diced

3 celery stalks, diced
12 garlic cloves, minced Sea Salt

Black pepper

1 16-ounce bag borlotti beans, rinsed and picked through2 28-ounce cans crushed tomatoes

5 cups vegetable broth1 bay leaf

2 tablespoons dried basil

2 teaspoons dried parsley

1 teaspoon coarse sea salt

1/2 – 1 teaspoon crushed red pepper flakes

Combine the onion, carrot, celery and garlic thoroughly and seasonwith salt and pepper.

Add in the remaining ingredients and stir thoroughly

Cook on low for 4 and a half hours, or until lentils begin to softenand sauce becomes thick.

Adjust seasoning by adding more salt & pepper to taste.

Vegetarian Brown Rice Burrito Bowl

Ingredients

1 red onion, diced or thinly sliced

1 green bell pepper (I used yellow), diced

¼ cup gouda cheese, shredded 1 mild red chili, finely chopped 1 ½ cups black beans, drained 1 cup uncooked brown rice

1 ½ cups chopped tomatoes

½ cup water

1 tbsp chipotle hot sauce (or other favorite hot sauce) 1 tsp smoked paprika

1/2 tsp ground cumin Sea salt

Black pepper

Toppings fresh coriander (cilantro), chopped spring onions,

sliced avocado, guacamole, etc.

Combine all the burrito bowl ingredients (not toppings) in a slowcooker.

Cook on low for 3 hours, or until the rice is cooked.

Serve hot with coriander, spring onions, avocado and guacamole.

Red Bean Burrito Bowl with Chimichurri Sauce

Ingredients

1 ancho chili, diced 1 red onion, diced

1 mild red chili, finely chopped 1 1/2 cup red beans

1 cup uncooked white rice

1 1/2 cups chopped tomatoes 1/2 cup water

4 tbsp. chimichurri sauce 1/2 tsp. cayenne pepper Sea salt

Black pepper

Toppings: fresh coriander (cilantro), chopped spring onions, sliced avocado, guacamole, etc.

Combine all the burrito bowl ingredients (not toppings) in a slowcooker.

Cook on low for 3 hours, or until the rice is cooked. Serve hot with topping ingredients

Garbanzo Bean Burrito Bowl with Sun-dried Pesto

Ingredients

5 jalapeno peppers, diced1 red onion, diced

1 mild red chili, finely chopped

1 ½ cups garbanzo beans, drained1 cup uncooked red rice

1 ½ cups chopped tomatoes

½ cup water

4 tbsp. sun-dried tomato pesto1 tsp. Italian seasoning

Sea salt
Black
pepper

Toppings: fresh coriander (cilantro), chopped spring onions, slicedavocado, guacamole, etc.

Combine all the burrito bowl ingredients (not toppings) in a slowcooker.

Cook on low for 3 hours, or until the rice is cooked. Serve hot with topping ingredients

Black Rice Burrito Bowl with Vegan Chorizos

Ingredients

5 Serrano peppers, diced 1 red onion, diced

1 mild red chili, finely chopped 1 1/2 cup navy beans, drained 1 cup uncooked black rice

1 1/2 cup chopped green tomatoes 1/2 cup water

1/4 cup vegan chorizos, coarsely chopped 1 tsp. dried thyme

Sea salt

Black

pepper

Toppings: fresh coriander (cilantro), chopped spring onions, sliced avocado, guacamole, etc.

Combine all the burrito bowl ingredients (not toppings) in a slowcooker.

Cook on low for 3 hours, or until the rice is cooked. Serve hot with topping ingredients

White Bean Vegetarian Burrito Bowl

Ingredients

1 Anaheim pepper, diced 1 red onion, diced

1 mild red chili, finely chopped 1 1/2 cup white beans

1 cup uncooked white rice

1 1/2 cups chopped tomatoes 1/2 cup water

4 tbsp. pepper jack cheese, shredded 1 tsp. herbs de Provence

Sea salt
Black
pepper

Toppings: fresh coriander (cilantro), chopped spring onions, sliced avocado, guacamole, etc.

Combine all the burrito bowl ingredients (not toppings) in a slowcooker.

Cook on low for 3 hours, or until the rice is cooked. Serve hot with topping ingredients

Vegetarian Chimichurri Burrito Bowl

Ingredients

1 red onion, diced or thinly sliced

1 green bell pepper (I used yellow),
diced1 mild red chili, finely chopped

1 ½ cups black beans, drained

1 cup Vegan Italian sausage, coarsely chopped 1 cup uncooked brown rice

1 ½ cups chopped tomatoes

½ cup water

4 tbsp. chimichurri sauce 1/2 tsp. cayenne pepper Sea salt

Black pepper

Toppings: fresh coriander (cilantro), chopped spring onions, sliced avocado, guacamole, etc.

Combine all the burrito bowl ingredients (not toppings) in a slow cooker.

Cook on low for 3 hours, or until the rice is cooked. Serve hot with topping ingredients

Vegetarian Garbanzo Bean Burrito Bowl

Ingredients

1 red onion, diced or thinly sliced

1 green bell pepper (I used yellow), diced 1 mild red chili, finely chopped

1 ½ cups garbanzo beans, drained 1 cup uncooked red rice

1 ½ cups chopped San Marzano tomatoes

½ cup water

1 tbsp chipotle hot sauce (or other favorite hot sauce) 1 tsp smoked paprika

1/2 tsp ground cumin Sea salt

Black pepper

Toppings: fresh coriander (cilantro), chopped spring onions, sliced avocado, guacamole, etc.

Combine all the burrito bowl ingredients (not toppings) in a slowcooker.

Cook on low for 3 hours, or until the rice is cooked. Serve hot with topping ingredients

Vegetarian Black Rice Burrito Bowl

Ingredients

1 poblano chili, diced 1 red onion, diced

1 mild red chili, finely chopped 1 1/2 cup navy beans, drained 1 cup uncooked black rice

1 1/2 cup chopped green tomatoes 1/2 cup water

8 tbsp. pesto

1 tsp. Italian seasoning Sea salt

Black pepper

Toppings: fresh coriander (cilantro), chopped spring onions, sliced avocado, guacamole, etc.

Combine all the burrito bowl ingredients (not toppings) in a slowcooker.

Cook on low for 3 hours, or until the rice is cooked. Serve hot with topping ingredients

White Bean and Ricotta Cheese Burrito Bowl

Ingredients

1 ancho chili, diced 1 red onion, diced

1 mild red chili, finely chopped 1 1/2 cup white beans

1 cup uncooked white rice

1 1/2 cups chopped tomatoes 1/2 cup water

8 tbsp. Ricotta cheese, sliced thinly 1 tsp. herbs de Provence

Sea salt
Black
pepper

Toppings: fresh coriander (cilantro), chopped spring onions, sliced avocado, guacamole, etc.

Combine all the burrito bowl ingredients (not toppings) in a slowcooker.

Cook on low for 3 hours, or until the rice is cooked. Serve hot with topping ingredients

Brown Rice with Vegetarian Sausage and Black Bean BurritoBowl

Ingredients

5 jalapeno peppers, diced 1 red onion, diced

1 mild red chili, finely chopped 1 ½ cups black beans, drained 1 cup uncooked brown rice

1 ½ cups chopped tomatoes

½ cup water

1/4 cup vegetarian grain meat sausage (brand: Field Roast), coarsely chopped

1 tsp. dried thyme Sea salt

Black pepper

Toppings: fresh coriander (cilantro), chopped spring onions,

sliced avocado, guacamole, etc.

Combine all the burrito bowl ingredients (not toppings) in a slow cooker.

Cook on low for 3 hours, or until the rice is cooked. Serve hot with topping ingredients

Red Rice and Garbanzo Beans with Chimichurri Sauce

Ingredients

5 Serrano peppers, diced1 red onion, diced

1 mild red chili, finely chopped

1 ½ cups garbanzo beans, drained

1/2 cup vegan burger (Brand: Beyond Meat Beyond Burger),crumbled

1 cup uncooked red rice

1 ½ cups chopped tomatoes

½ cup water

4 tbsp. chimichurri sauce1/2 tsp. cayenne pepper Sea salt

Black pepper

Toppings: fresh coriander (cilantro), chopped spring onions,

sliced avocado, guacamole, etc.

Combine all the burrito bowl ingredients (not toppings) in a slow cooker.

Cook on low for 3 hours, or until the rice is cooked. Serve hot with topping ingredients

Conclusion

We have now reached the end of this fantastic cookbook, I hope it has been to your liking and has met your expectations.

Our book of soups besides being great for leaking ideas for our dishes also cares about our physical fitness, in fact in order to reap all the benefits of the vegetarian diet I would also recommend some physical activity so as to achieve the right balance between body and spirit.

I send you a big hug and hope to keep you company with our vegetarian recipes.

9 781667 167251